THE PRAIRIE

BIOMES

Lynn M. Stone

The Rourke Corporation, Inc.
Vero Beach, Florida 32964

PHOTO CREDITS
All photos © Lynn M. Stone

Library of Congress Cataloging-in-Publication Data
Stone, Lynn M.
    The prairie / by Lynn M. Stone.
        p.   cm. — (Biomes)
    Includes index.
    Summary: Describes the prairie of central North America including the grasses, other plants, birds, mammals, and life underground.
    ISBN 0-86593-420-7
    1. Prairie ecology—Juvenile literature. 2. Prairies—Juvenile literature. [1. Prairie ecology. 2. Ecology. 3. Prairies.] I. Title. II. Series: Stone, Lynn M. Biomes.
QH541.5.P7S75   1996
574.5'2643—dc20   95-46186
                                            CIP
                                             AC

Printed in the USA

CL
4/98

TABLE OF CONTENTS

The Prairie   5
Prairie Grasses   6
Other Prairie Plants   9
Life on the Prairie   11
Life Under the Prairie   14
Prairie Birds   16
Prairie Mammals   19
Visiting the Prairies   20
Protecting the Prairie   22
Glossary   23
Index   24

THE PRAIRIE

The open, almost treeless **prairie** (PRAYR ee) was central North America's sea of grass. It waved and rippled in the wind for as far as anyone could see.

The prairie grasses stretched from central Texas to southern Saskatchewan, Canada. The prairie rolled like a carpet of green and bronze from Illinois and Missouri west to the Rockies.

Much of the prairie has been plowed or turned into pasture. Prairie lands today are scattered and scarce.

A pronghorn stands in a sea of Dakota grasses

PRAIRIE GRASSES

Grasses are the most important plants of the prairies. They can be a few inches tall, or several feet tall. Less rain falls on the western prairies, so their grasses are shorter than eastern prairie grasses.

In the wetter, eastern prairies of Kansas, Nebraska, Iowa, and Illinois, big bluestem and cordgrass grow to be six and seven feet tall!

Wild prairie grasses have dense, deep roots. The roots help keep trees from finding a place to grow.

The prairies are a blanket of deep-rooted grasses and other wild plants

OTHER PRAIRIE PLANTS

The roots, stems, and leaves of wildflowers help make the thick prairie mat of plants. Like the grasses, prairie wildflowers are made to survive heat, cold, **drought** (DROWT) — and even fire.

The prairies begin to bloom in March. By the Fourth of July, and into September, they are colorful wild gardens. Tall, yellow sunflowers and dock stretch above orange lilies, white orchids, blue asters, purple gentians, and pink roses.

A few trees — oaks, aspens, willows — live along prairie streams.

Purple prairie clover brightens the grassland in summer

LIFE ON THE PRAIRIE

Prairie plants grow from the **nourishment** (NOOR ish ment) of air, sunlight, and soil. The plants support animal life on the prairie.

A prairie dog, for example, eats plants. A coyote, falcon, or ferret may then eat the prairie dog. In that way, food energy moves from the plant to the animal.

Many **predators** (PRED uh torz), or meat-eaters, live on the prairies. They may be as small as robber flies or as large as mountain lions.

A prairie dog, which is really a ground squirrel, fattens up on the prairie plants around its burrow

A burrowing owl preys on prairie insects and other small animals

The prairie rattlesnake hunts rabbits, ground squirrels, and other small prey on the western grasslands

LIFE UNDER THE PRAIRIE

With no forest hiding places, many prairie animals make their homes *under* the sea of grass. The prairies are great places for burrowers — or diggers — like beetles, moles, kit foxes, burrowing owls, badgers, and prairie dogs.

Prairie dogs live in "towns" of burrows. Some of their towns cover many square miles, like human towns!

Prairie dogs spend much of their lives underground. They have several tunnels and "rooms."

A cousin of the weasel and otter, the badger is a prairie predator and master digger

PRAIRIE BIRDS

Prairie plants and insects are food for many birds. Franklin's gulls, for example, love to snack on grasshoppers. Bobolinks, meadowlarks, sparrows, and blackbirds gobble insects, too.

Prairie lakes and marshes draw hundreds of thousands of water birds to their shores and islands. Ducks, geese, swans, shorebirds, cranes, **grebes** (GREEBZ), and white pelicans nest in these prairie **wetlands** (WET landz).

The loud cries of water birds in flight are prairie music each spring and fall.

Once common, the prairie chicken became rare as its prairie home began to quickly disappear

PRAIRIE MAMMALS

The prairie's furry creatures are good burrowers or runners. Being able to dig or run can be life-saving on the open prairies.

Big bison don't look like they could dig *or* run. Their only digging is pawing out shallow dust baths. However, bison can run — up to 40 miles per hour.

The pronghorn of the western prairies is even faster. Next to the cheetah, it is the fastest land animal.

Big and brawny, a bison bull tramples through a prairie dog town in South Dakota

VISITING THE PRAIRIES

You can find bits and pieces of prairie in Ohio west into Wyoming. Three of the largest old prairies are the Flint Hills of Kansas, and Badlands National Park and Custer State Park of South Dakota.

The eastern prairies, especially in Wisconsin and Illinois, have many kinds of plants. A few of the western prairies, such as Wind Cave National Park in South Dakota, still have prairie dog towns, bison, and pronghorns.

Visitors can enjoy the sights and sounds of old prairie at Wind Cave National Park in South Dakota

PROTECTING THE PRAIRIE

Much of the American West is grassland. However, little of it is the way it was in the days of Sitting Bull and General George Custer. Some North American grassland is not true prairie. It has grasses that weren't in the prairie before. Some prairies have been nibbled away by cattle and sheep.

Several small pieces of old prairie, though, are being saved. People are also planting prairie plants to **restore** (re STORE) or remake, small prairies.

Glossary

drought (DROWT) — a period of little, or no, rainfall

grebe (GREEB) — a sharp-billed diving bird of ponds and lakes

nourishment (NOOR ish ment) — food for growth and healthy living

prairie (PRAYR ee) — a treeless, grassy area that can be damp or dry; the natural grassland of west central North America

predator (PRED uh tor) — an animal that kills other animals for food

restore (re STORE) — make something like it used to be

wetland (WET land) — a low, wet area covered by shallow water for at least part of the year; a marsh, bog, or swamp

INDEX

Badlands National
    Park, SD   20
birds   16
    water   16
bison   19, 20
burrowers   14, 19
burrows   14
Custer State Park, SD   20
Flint Hills, KS   20
grasses   5, 6, 9, 22
    big bluestem   6
    cordgrass   6
insects   16
lakes   16
marshes   16

plants   11, 16, 22
prairie dog   11, 20
predators   11
pronghorns   19, 20
rainfall   6
roots   6
trees   6, 9
wetlands   16
wildflowers   9
Wind Cave National
    Park, SD   20